Canny Manny and Kipper Cat

Claire Donald

ISBN: 9781838166526

Typeset by Funny Onion Stories www.FunnyOnionStories.com
A catalogue for this book is available from the British Library.

Funny Onion Stories

www.FunnyOnionStories.com

To Mam with love.

Every night when the clock struck twelve, Canny Manny met Kipper Cat.

They strolled around the town and had their usual nightly chat.

But tonight as they walked down the high street, something made them stop.

They could see a burglar stealing things from inside the jewellery shop.

The Glitterati

“My goodness!” exclaimed Kipper Cat, “what ever shall we do?”

You’re the clever one Canny Manny; I’ll leave it up to you.”

Canny Manny thought for a while then said, “I have a plan.

I believe the vehicle parked in the lane must be the getaway van.”

The Glitterati
B1LL
Manny

“Listen carefully Kipper Cat, this is my idea.

It’s really quite simple my feline friend, nothing for you to fear.

As soon as the burglar gets into his van, you must jump on to the roof.

He will drive back home with the jewels, then we go to the police with proof.”

Police
Station
Manny

"That's fine" said Kipper Cat, "but when we get to the station.

How will we tell the police all of the information? "

"Leave that to me," Canny Manny replied. "Now go and hide in the lane."

"But what if I fall?" asked Kipper Cat, "and die in terrible pain?"

“Don’t be silly ” said Canny Manny, “cats are lithe and agile.”

“But I’m not like that,” sighed Kipper Cat, “I’m clumsy and ever so fragile.

I know people say we have nine lives, but I really don’t know if that’s true.

But if it is: I have probably already lost quite a few.”

“Come on,” said Canny Manny, “I have a cunning notion.

I’ll bark and bark very loudly and scare him with all the commotion.

He will run out through the door and drive off in the van.

All you have to do Kipper Cat is hold on as tight as you can.”

B1LL
Manny

“You need to look very carefully and remember the route you took.

Come back and tell me where it is, then I will take a look.

I’ll have a sniff around and think of another plan.

So the police will know just where to find that naughty burglar man.”

Manny

Canny Manny stood by the shop, and barked with all his might.

And just as he had predicted, the burglar man took flight.

He jumped into his van and sped off very fast.

Canny Manny held his breath as Kipper Cat whizzed past.

Manny

After a little while, the van suddenly came to a halt.

Kipper Cat shot off the roof and did a somersault!

He picked himself up off the very hard ground, with a little trepidation.

Then, he looked at his surroundings to remember the location.

16
B1LL

At last Kipper Cat found his way back to the jewellery shop in town.

Canny Manny was still in the doorway having a little lie down.

“Quick get up” shouted Kipper Cat, “before I forget the way.”

Then off they ran as fast as they could before night turned into day.

Manny

When they got to the burglar's house, Canny Manny revealed his plan.

Then they waited until morning, when the postman came in his van.

The postman walked to the door and was ready to post the mail.

When suddenly! Canny Manny, through the air did sail.

16
Post
Mr Burgla Bill
6 High Court Terrace
North Pentonville.

He bit into the letter, the postman screamed and let go.

Then Canny Manny sped off, with Kipper Cat in tow.

They ran as fast as they could, back to the scene of the crime.

They got to the jewellery shop, just in the nick of time.

Post

The police were in the jewellery shop, and one officer stood in the street.

So Canny Manny and Kipper Cat sat at the officer's feet.

"What's that you have in your mouth?" she asked, as she gently took it out.

She read the name and address on the letter, then gave her colleagues a shout.

The Glitterati
1256
1256
Mr Burglar Bill
16 High Court Terrace
North Pentonville.

“Come and see what I have, you are in for a big surprise! “

When the others saw the letter they could not believe their eyes.

“The envelope is clearly addressed to Mr Burglar Bill.

16 High Court Terrace, North Pentonville.”

2583
2583
1256
1256
Mr Burglar Bill
16 High Court Terrace
North Pentonville
Manny

“The culprit must have lost it as he left the jewellery shop.

Luckily for us it seems he did not hear it drop.

This clever dog and clever cat delivered the letter to me.

Let’s go to this address as quickly as can be...”

1256

Burglar Bill was arrested and put in a prison cell.

The swag was returned to the jewellery shop and the door was fixed as well.

Canny Manny and Kipper Cat were lauded and applauded.

And both of our very brave heroes were handsomely rewarded.

CONGRATULATIONS

Comprehension Questions

What time did Canny Manny and Kipper Cat meet each night?

Why did Kipper Cat think Canny Manny's plan would not work?

How do you think Kipper Cat felt about it all?

Why do you think Kipper Cat had to go on the van instead of Canny Manny?

What number house did Burglar Bill live in?

How do you think the man delivering the post felt? Why do you think that?

What was Canny Manny thinking when everyone was applauding?

Printed in Great Britain
by Amazon

72850839R00022